Discussion Book for Children:

A, B, C of things kids would want to know about dogs

Leatrice Yoshie

Edited by Yoko Mogi-Hein, EdD

Dedicated to Beanie, my loving dog

Midori Press / Tokyo / An Imprint of Midori Co.

LIBRARY OF CONGRESS CATALOGING-IN-PUBLICATION DATA

ISBN-13: 978-1513631141 (Amazon.com)
ISBN-10: 1513631144

"A" is for Akita

Akita's Life Expectancy: 10-13 years
Personality: Courageous and loyal to children and pet parents
Energy Level: Not a hyper breed, but Akita dogs enjoy regular exercise
Good with Children: Better with supervision
Good with other Dogs: Not recommended
Shedding: Seasonal / **Grooming:** Weekly
Trainability: Eager to please / **Height:** 24-28 inches
Weight: 70-130 pounds / **Barking Level:** Quiet

"A" is for Always - remember that your dog has feelings:

Dogs feel—they have emotions and they understand emotions. Recent scientific studies have shown that dogs experience love like humans and can read human emotions based on facial expressions (American Kennel Club, 2017). Dogs have the capacity to love, feel, become depressed and get excited.

"B" is for Beagle

Beagle's Life Expectancy: 10-15 years
Personality: Sweet, friendly, and curious
Shedding: Seasonal / **Grooming:** Weekly
Energy Level: Very Active; Beagles needs plenty of exercise
Good with Children: Yes / **Good with other Dogs:** Yes
Trainability: Responds well /**Height:** 13-15 inches
Weight: 20-30 pounds / **Barking Level**: Likes to be loud and vccal

"B" is for Be careful -

Do not leave a dog alone in the car the warmer months, a car can cause your dog to become extremely overheated and sick. If left alone for too long, a dog can even die. In the winter months, a car acts as a refrigerator and can have equally scary consequences. And no matter the weather or season, a dog alone in a car is a target for thieves. Dogs should never be left alone in a vehicle unattended.

"C" is for Chihuahua

Chihuahua's Life Expectancy: 12-20 years
Personality: Graceful, charming, and wise.
Energy Level: High and playful but they are mostly an indoor pet.
Good with Children: Better with older children
Good with other Dogs: Good with supervision
Shedding: Seasonal / **Grooming:** Weekly brushing
Trainability: Independent
Height: 6 - 10 inches / **Weight:** 3 -15 pounds
Barking Level: Barks when necessary

"C" is for Care: Chihuahua dogs can live a very long life. Some can live

20 years. But these small dogs need lots of love and attention from their pet owners. When they are puppies, they need to be taught by their pet owners what is acceptable at home and outside. Chihuahua dogs are just like small children.

"D" is for Dachshund

Dachshund's Life Expectancy: 12-16 years
Personality: Happy and spunky
Energy Level: Active so it's good to keep him busy
Good with Children: Better with supervision
Good with other Dogs: With supervision
Shedding: Seasonal / **Grooming:** Weekly brushing
Trainability: Responds Well
Height: 8-9 inches (standard), 5-6 inches (miniature)
Weight: 16-32 lb /**Barking Level:** Barks loud when necessary

"D" is for Don't. Please don't forget to brush your dog's teeth:
Always have a veterinarian check your dog's teeth at least once a year. Get into the habit of regular dental care and treats that cleans their teeth. Never use human toothpaste on a dog. Why? They can't spit, and there are ingredients in many human toothpastes that can make a dog sick.

"E" is for English Cocker Spaniel

Life Expectancy: 12-14 years
Personality: Responsive, active with energy
Energy Level: Active; Upbeat outdoors, mellow indoors
Good with Children: Yes
Good with other Dogs: Yes
Shedding: Seasonal
Grooming: Weekly
Trainability: Eager To Please
Height: 16-17 inches (male), 15-16 inches (female)
Weight: 28-34 pounds (male), 26-32 pounds (female)
Barking Level: Barks When Necessary

"E" is for Eating.

Dog needs to eat healthy food for dogs, not the human food.

"F" is for French bulldog

French Bulldog's Life Expectancy: 10-12 years
Personality: Playful, smart, adaptable, and irresistible
Energy Level: Not Very Active; Frenchies are easygoing, not terribly athletic; brisk walks will keep them trim
Good with Children: Yes
Good with other Dogs: With Supervision
Shedding: Seasonal
Grooming: Occasional
Trainability: Responds Well
Height: 11-13 inches
Weight: under 28 pounds
Barking Level: Quiet

"F" is for Freedom. Your dog enjoys freedom to play with you. Spend some time everyday with your dog at home and outside. You can also teach your dog a trick or two!

"G" is for German Shepherd

German Shepherd's Life Expectancy: 7-10 years
Personality: Smart, confident, courageous, and steady
Energy Level: Very Active; they require regular exercise
Good with Children: Yes
Good with other Dogs: With supervision
Shedding: Frequent / **Grooming:** Occasional
Trainability: Eager To Please
Height: 24-26 inches (male), 22-24 inches (female)
Weight: 65-90 pounds (male), 50-70 pounds (female)
Barking Level: Barks When Necessary

"G" is for Give.
Give your dog the freedom to be a bit wild and dirty. It makes your dog very happy to be outside having fun with you.

" H" is for Hokkaido

Have you met a Hokkaido dog? The Hokkaido, also known as **Ainu** dog is one of the newest dog breed recorded in the American Kennel Club (2016) and in the Foundation Stock Service since January, 2016 (Federation Cynologique Internationale, 2017).

Hokkaido's Life Expectancy: 7-10 years
Personality: Alert, bold, faithful, and dignified
Energy Level: Very Active; they require regular exercise
Good with Children: Yes
Good with other Dogs: With supervision
Shedding: Frequent / **Grooming:** Occasional
Trainability: Eager To Please / **Height:** 20-24 inches
Weight: 50-70 lb / **Barking Level:** Barks When Necessary

"H"is for Hitting. Hitting a dog is wrong: It will harm your relationship with your dog and your ability to train (Paw Culture, 2017).

"I" is for Italian Hound

Italian Hound Life Expectancy: 14-15 years
Personality: Sensitive and alert, playful, highly affectionate
Energy Level: Somewhat Active; they like to ran and dash
Good with Children: Better with older children
Good with other Dogs: Yes
Shedding: Seasonal
Grooming: Occasional
Trainability: Responds Well
Height: 13-15 inches
Weight: 7-14 pounds
Barking Level: Barks When Necessary

"I" is for If. If you treat your dog well, she will be your best friend forever.

"J" is for Japanese Chin

Japanese Chin's Personality: Charming but quiet with strangers

Energy Level: Somewhat Active; Love walking and learning tricks

Good with Children: Better with older children
Good with other Dogs: Yes
Shedding: Seasonal
Grooming: Occasional
Trainability: Independent
Height: 8-11 inches
Weight: 7-11 pounds
Barking Level: Quiet

"J" is for _____.

Write a teaching message here.

"K" is for Komondore

Komondore's Life Expectancy: 10-12 years
Personality: Dignified, brave, protective, steadfastly loyal
Energy Level: Very active;
 Without a big, fenced-in area to patrol, dog needs walks daily
Good with Children: Better with older children
Good with other Dogs: Not recommended
Shedding: Seasonal / **Grooming:** Daily
Trainability: Responds Well
Height: 27.5 minimum inches (male), 25.5 minimum inches (female)
Weight: 80- 100 pounds or more
Barking Level: Barks When Necessary

"K" is for

_____.Write a

teaching message here.

"**L**" is for Labrador Retriever

Labrador Retriever's Life Expectancy: 10-12 years
Personality: Friendly and outgoing, Labs play well with others
Energy Level: Very Active; Labs are high-spirited
Good with Children: Yes / **Good with other Dogs:** Yes.
Shedding: Seasonal / **Grooming:** Occasional
Trainability: Eager To Please
Height: 21-25 inches / **Weight:** 55-80 pounds
Barking Level: Barks When Necessary

"L" is for love. Labrador Retriever from Canada continues to be the most liked breed in the United States, according to American Kennel Club registration statistics. This versatile hunting breed comes in three colors - yellow, black and chocolate - and because of their desire to please their master, they excel as guide dogs for the blind, as part of search-and-rescue teams or in narcotics detection with law enforcement.

" M " is for Maltese

Maltese's Life Expectancy: 12-15 years
Personality: Gentle, playful, affectionate
Energy Level: Active; A classic lapdog but like walks
Good with Children: Better with older children
Good with other Dogs: With supervision
Shedding: Infrequent
Grooming: Weekly
Trainability: Responds Well
Height: 8-10 inches
Weight: 6-8 pounds
Barking Level: Barks When Necessary

"M" is for _____.
Write a teaching message here.

"N" is for Neapolitan Mastif

Neapolitan Mastif's Life Expectancy: 7-9 years
Personality: Watchful and sweet but wary with strangers
Energy Level: Not Very Active; This placid, lumbering dog shouldbe walked a few times a day
Good with Children: Better with Supervision
Good with other Dogs: With Supervision
Shedding: Seasonal / **Grooming:** Occasional
Trainability: Independent / **Height:** 24-31 inches
Weight: 150 pounds / **Barking Level:** Barks When Necessary

"N" is for Never. Never use the kennel for timeouts to punish your dog. Unlike children, timeouts don't work for dogs. If a dog gets jumpy or excessively barks, putting him in a kennel is wrong. In fact, the dog just learned that the kennel is a bad place. If you love your dog, you should never forget.

"O" is for Old English Sheep Dog

Old English Sheep Dog's Life Expectancy: 10-12 years
Personality: Adaptable, smart, and gentle
Energy Level: Somewhat Active; A mellow house dog but dog likes long walks, and a good gallop
Good with Children: Better with supervision
Good with other Dogs: With Supervision
Shedding: Seasonal / **Grooming:** Weekly
Trainability: Responds Well
Height: 22 inches & up / **Weight:** 60-100 pounds
Barking Level: Barks When Necessary

"O" is for _____.
Write a teaching message here.

"P" is for Pug

Pug's Life Expectancy: 13-15 years
Personality: Even-tempered, charming, and loving
Energy Level: Somewhat Active; Pugs are not exactly natural athletes, but they do have strong legs and endless curiosity—exercise both regularly
Good with Children: Better with Supervision
Good with other Dogs: With supervision
Shedding: Seasonal / **Grooming:** Occasional
Trainability: Responds well / **Height:** 10-13 inches
Weight: 14-18 pounds / **Barking Level:** Barks When Necessary

"P" is for People.
People are born to learn how to lead a good life and be a good person everyday. Dogs already know how to do this. That's why they don't need to live so long. If you love your dog, you should never forget.

"Q" is for Quiet time. There is no dog breed that begins with "Q".

Draw a picture of your favorite dog here.

"Q" is for_____.

Write a teaching message here.

"R" is for Rottweiler

Personality: Reserved with strangers and affectionate and loyal with his family.
Energy Level: The Rottie needs at least two solid workouts daily;he would really appreciate it if these always included you!
Good with Children: Better with Supervision
Good with other Dogs: With Supervision
Shedding: Seasonal / **Grooming:** Occasional
Trainability: Responds Well
Height: 24-27 inches (male), 22-25 inches (female)
Weight: 110-130 pounds (male), 77-110 pounds (female)
Life Expectancy: 8-10 years
Barking Level: Barks When Necessary

"R" is for Remembering. Remember these words... your dog will always love you no matter what.

"S" is for Saint Bernard

Saint Bernard's Life Expectancy: 8-10 years
Personality: Friendly, patient, outgoing
Energy Level: Not Very Active; A mature Saint will be content with long walks and a romp on the lawn
Good with Children: Yes
Good with other Dogs: With Supervision
Shedding: Seasonal
Grooming: Occasional
Trainability: Responds Well
Height: 28-30 inches (males), 26-28 inches (female)
Weight: 140-180 pounds (male), 120-140 pounds (female)
Barking Level: Barks When Necessary

"S" is for showing. Show your dog that humans are loving and are not mean and violent. If you love your dog, you should never forget.

"T" is for Tibetan Mastiff

Tibetan Mastiff's Life Expectancy: 12-15 years
Personality: Mellow and calm around the house; devoted to family, reserved and territorial with strangers.
Energy Level: Enjoy exercise in all weather
Good with Children: Yes
Good with other Dogs: With supervision
Shedding: Seasonal / **Grooming:** Occasional
Trainability: Independent / **Height:** 24-30 inches
Weight: 75-160 pounds
Barking Level: Barks when necessary

"T" is for is for

_____. Write a
teaching message here.

"U" is Understanding. There is no dog breed that begins with "U".

Draw a picture of your favorite dog here.

"U" is for is for

_____. Write a

teaching message here.

"V" is for Vizsla

Personality: Gentle, affectionate, energetic and eager
Energy Level: Very Active
Good with other Dogs: With Supervision
Shedding: Seasonal / **Grooming:** Occasional
Trainability: Eager To Please
Height: 12-24 inches / **Weight:** 44-60 pounds
Life Expectancy: 12-14 years
Barking Level: Barks When Necessary

"V" is for is for

_____. Write a

teaching message here.

"W" is for Whippet

Whippet's Life Expectancy: 12-15 years
Personality: Calm, affectionate, and playful
Energy Level: Somewhat Active; This breed has spurts of energetic moments followed by a lazy afternoon
Good with Children: Better with Supervision
Good with other Dogs: Yes
Shedding: Seasonal / **Grooming:** Occasional
Trainability: Responds Well
Height: 19-22 inches (male), 18-21 inches (female)
Weight: 25-40 pounds / **Barking Level:** Quiet

"W" is for When. When your dog gets old, please love her as much as you did when she was a puppy.

" X" is for Xoloitzcuintli

Xoloitzcuintli or "Xolo" in short, is the first dog of the Americas. Their name came two thousand years ago from the Aztec Indian god, Xolotl and Itzcuintli, the Aztec word for dog (American Kennel Club, 2017).

Xolo's Life Expectancy: 13-18 years
Personality: Loyal, alert, calm, good watchdog
Energy Level: Somewhat Active; Xolos like long walks
Good with Children: Better with Supervision
Good with other Dogs: With Supervision
Shedding: Infrequent, Hypoallergenic
Grooming: Occasional / **Trainability:** Responds Well
Height: 18-23 inches / **Weight:** 30-55 pounds
Barking Level: Barks When Necessary

"X" is for _____.
Write a teaching message here.

"Y" is for Yorkshire Terrier

Life Expectancy: 11-15 years
Yorkshire Terriers' Personality: Cheerful and affectionate
Energy Level: Active; Very happy with a daily satisfying walk
Good with Children: Better with Supervision
Good with other Dogs: With Supervision
Shedding: Infrequent
Grooming: Daily
Trainability: Independent
Height: 7-8 inches / **Weight:** 7 pounds
Barking Level: Barks When Necessary

"Y" for is for _____.

Write a teaching message here.

"Z" is for Zest.

There is no dog breed that begins with **"Z"**. It's fine because all dogs have **"Z" for zest, and zest for life.** What is zest? Zest is a joy and great energy. Let's do all the good we can, in all the ways we can, in all the places we can, at all the times we can, to all the dogs we can, as long as we can so that we will all enjoy their zest for life. Let's take good care of them for a long, long time. *~Leatrice Yoshie Hein*

Educational Activities

1. Sing a song about dog together.

   Suggested songs: Bingo, Old McDonald Had A Farm

2. Match picture and dog name for young children

3. Match picture and dog description for older children

4. Draw a picture of dog together (children and mom / teacher)

5. Follow-Up Discussion Questions: **Topics suggested for the parent and child. Conversation after the read aloud:**

   - **Think Dog:** understanding your pup

   - **Talk Dog:** canine communication

   - **Dog School:** basic obedience training

   - **Dog's Dinner:** the right diet

   - **Accidents Will Happen:** house-training

   - **You'll Never Walk Alone:** exercise

Acknowledgements

The year was 2010. My family and I moved to Edwardsville, Illinois and one weekend volunteering for a humane society in town. We became a regular volunteer for walking dogs there on weekends that summer. I remember meeting wonderful staff and volunteers there. Seven years later, in the summer of 2017, I am very excited that I am putting together this children's book for my Girl Scouts Gold Service Leadership project.

As a young child, I have always loved animals. Among others, I enjoy the companionship of my dog at home. Children enjoy learning about dogs and that they are capable of learning about positive and responsible dog ownership behaviors. I would like to make a difference in the lives of dogs and their owners in our community by reducing neglect and abuse.

This book is dedicated to my loving dog, Beanie and two organizations that advocate for well-being of dogs locally and globally. The first organization is the American Kennel Club - a national organization headquartered in St.Louis, Missouri, and the second organization is the Metro East Humane Society - a local animal shelter in Edwardsville, Illinois. In particular, I would like to thank the following individuals and families for their generous assistance and support; Ms. Cheryl Heimer, Ms. Courtney Schaefer, Ms. Mary Buchanan, Ms. Liz Link, my friend, Sydney Joslyn and volunteers, friends, troop leaders, and other members of the Girl Scouts of Southern Illinois Troop 52, Mrs. Karen Martin and my parents.

The image courtesy for all dogs in this book with two exceptions go to the American Kennel Club dog breeds at http://www.akc.org/dog-breeds. The image of a German Shepherd dog, courtesy of Nette Eriksson at Pixabay.com provided a public statement in CC0 Creative Commons: Free for commercial use and no attribution required. The last image courtesy of Beanie on the cover page goes to my brother, William.

Leatrice Yoshie

About Author:

Leatrice Yoshie is a young writer and an animal enthusiast. She lives with her family in Edwardsville, Illinois.

About Editor:

Yoko Mogi-Hein, EdD is a Senior Lecturer at University of Wisconsin - Oshkosh, specializing in Curriculum and Instruction. She writes and publishes scholarly work on pedagogy. She was a 2017 Corwin Fellow at Teachers College, Columbia University's Cowin Financial Literacy Institute.

www.ingramcontent.com/pod-product-compliance
Lightning Source LLC
Chambersburg PA
CBHW042117040426

42449CB00002B/81